Playing T
Graduate Game

Welcome to the highest stakes game you've ever played
Welcome to the graduate game

Acknowledgements

Special thanks to Tim Driver: Arguably the slowest IT designer in the world, unarguably the finest. To all others that contributed to the making of this book: some of you made it better, some made it worse – together you made it what it is.

ISBN: 978-1-4092-0005-5

Printed and bound in Great Britain

Playing The Graduate Game

Guy Alexander Thornton

BA (Hons) Economics - University of Nottingham

Every morning in Africa, a gazelle wakes up. It knows it must run faster than the fastest lion or it will be killed. Every morning a lion wakes up. It knows it must outrun the slowest gazelle or it will starve. It doesn't matter whether you are a lion or a gazelle... when the sun comes up, you'd better be running.

African Proverb

INTRODUCTION

THE STATE OF PLAY

Life for the modern day graduate is unenviable; not only do we bid farewell to the fun of university, but we enter the world of work – or so we presume. Academically, graduates are highly successful, consistently finishing at the top of the charts. Yet rather than being headhunted as we might expect, we are thrown into the affray to battle for the elusive places on the top graduate schemes. As the flood of graduates increases yearly, the graduate job hunt becomes more exacting and the risk of being demoralised by the whole process becomes more real. The conventional graduate jobs in the professions and management have failed to expand at an equivalent rate to the explosion of new graduates. Recruiters now have a superior graduate base from which to choose with 20 times more graduates than positions.

To compound the problem, recruiters have recently emphasised their drive for diversity, moving recruiters away from the traditional hunting grounds of the red brick universities. Hiring candidates from lower rated universities substantiates their belief that the war for talent is about manifesting a managerial meritocracy, not just a way of reinforcing class advantages. The combination of more graduates competing for jobs and recruiters opening their positions to a wider range of graduates has amplified the competition for jobs to a new level.

With the competition fierce and the chances of getting a job low, why enter the notoriously arduous graduate recruitment process? The reason is that acquiring a job on a graduate scheme will take you a world apart from your peers, changing the future direction of your life. Not only will it affect your income and the assets you derive from your income; it will determine the finer contributors to your identity such as your status among friends and family, how fulfilled you are by your work and even the type of partner you will attract. The prospects you gain enable you to progress at a rate unparalleled by alternative jobs.

THE GAME

A common fallacy is that recruiters employ the best candidate for the job. Not only is this the view of the recruiters themselves, it is the view of many applicants. These candidates are 'preachers' - they genuinely believe what they preach throughout the recruitment process and have faith in their abilities to secure them a job. At the opposite end of the spectrum are the 'players' - graduates who appreciate all the hidden tests assessors perform and are prepared to modify as many of their attributes as it takes in order to get the jobs. Players understand that it is not the best candidate that gets the job; it is the candidate who most closely represents what the employers want to see. They appreciate that the recruitment process is a game that requires skills like any other game and they are willing to learn them. That is what this book is all about. It has taken me 2 years to learn how to play the graduate game but now that I have, I feel compelled to share what I learnt.

This book is the exact opposite of existing books in the graduate recruitment field, perhaps because it was written by someone who has been through the process, rather than a 'recruitment expert'. The first thing you must know is that it is a numbers game and as such, forget wasting your time trying to produce the perfect application. The rationale for this is that recruiters are too discriminatory and the recruitment process is too subjective for this to be worthwhile. Many graduate job books describe how to create the 'perfect CV' or how to 'blitz the interview' but this is a chronic waste of your time. It is not possible to get every job you apply for. Maybe the recruiter had a bad day, maybe they don't like northerners or maybe they asked ridiculous questions in the interview which you couldn't have prepared for. There are always going to be factors out of your control. Instead of following the perpetual road towards perfection, I will show you how to pass each stage quickly so you can apply to a multitude of firms.

Rather than spending weeks perfecting applications, you will learn how to complete successful applications in under an hour. Using these techniques to send multiple applications daily will all but guarantee you a top job. You might point out that you want a specific job, not just any graduate job. While getting a specific job can not be guaranteed, by submitting many applications you will gain practice and experience, increasing the likelihood of getting that specific job. It is also important to remember that there is really no point assigning too much value to any job before the application process. I found that the favourite job I was applying for changed three or four times during the full application process. The popular statements firms make about being innovators or market leaders make firms relatively indistinguishable. Only once you go through the application process do you gain any real knowledge of the firm you are applying to.

Despite the rather exhilarating nature of the content of this book, please refrain from reading it cover to cover in one sitting. The book is carefully designed to allow you just to read the section that coincides with the progress of your application. Magically, this focuses your attention on your current application stage and prevents you from wasting time reading a full book before you begin. As your application progresses, so you are invited to advance through the book to the corresponding chapter.

FROM PREACHER TO PLAYER

Unlike the majority of authors in this field I am not a recruiter, I am just a guy who has spent the last couple of years going through the whole process with varying levels of success. When I started applying, I read every cutting-edge graduate recruitment book on the market. I followed the books meticulously, creating the 'perfect CV' and became the gold standard on which to pit your graduate recruitment knowledge. I truly believed in the 'perfect application' and spent weeks endeavouring to achieve it, culminating in four complete applications. Three out of four passed the online application stage, then two out of three passed the psychometric tests, one out of two passed the telephone interview and on the one assessment day I had, I failed. This is a very typical graduate recruitment experience.

A year later, armed with a renewed motivation I left my comfortable university life once again to engage in the graduate recruitment process. After the failure of the year before, I decided to reject the so far useless advice of the 'recruitment experts' and unlearn everything. I incorporated a variety of new ideas and techniques. The more applications I submitted and the further they progressed, the clearer the science of the recruitment process became. Initially, half my online applications would be successful, then two thirds, then nine tenths. These pass percentages increased in other stages as well. I have now reached the point that I can apply for any graduate job I wish and have a very high chance of getting it. In fact, just yesterday I received two graduate job offers on the same day. I am not informing you of these thrilling stats to receive your accolades, I am telling you this to help demonstrate the massive level of success that can be achieved by following some simple guidelines. All the skills and techniques I have learnt can be taught and that is exactly what this book aims to achieve. The most important thing to remember is that the whole process is a game; to get good at it, you must learn how to play.

APPLICATION OVERVIEW

THE APPLICATION PROCESS

Gone is the auspicious era where your graduation certificate was a golden ticket to the world of work. The age of applying for a job by sending your C.V and cover letter is history. The relative increased supply of graduates to jobs means companies now have a much greater choice and can justify spending extra time trying to find exactly the right candidate for the job. It would be nice if recruiters had a little more faith in their talent spotting abilities. After all, recruiters used to hire graduates based on a CV and maybe an hour long interview. Unfortunately, since they make the rules, we must learn to play their game.

The application process usually comprises:

- Stage 1: Online application form
- Stage 2: Psychometric tests
- Stage 3: Telephone Interview or First Interview
- Stage 4: Assessment day

Please note that different firms do these stages in different orders. While one company may offer you an assessment day straight after the application process, others have tests and telephone interviews first. The key is to understand that while firms' application processes may seem different, they all comprise the same challenges and tests, masked in various disguises.

THE CHOICE OF JOBS

Deciding which job to pick is a beautifully simple process that people love to overcomplicate. As a graduate you are either qualified to perform or begin training to perform, almost any job. Therefore, don't pick your choice of career based on what you think you are most qualified to do. Sure, you have a better chance of being an accountant if you have done maths than psychology but you have a worse chance if the psychologist is keen and you are indifferent. Providing you have the necessary prerequisites, this book will enable you to get a job in any industry you desire. By picking an industry you favour, you will be more enthusiastic throughout the application process, increasing your chances of getting a job. The jobs you apply for should be based on your interests, values, motivations and the activities you enjoy. Your abilities should have little influence on your application as you will excel at the job you are interested in, value or are motivated to perform. You may wish to consider your long term prospects between particular industries but unless they are notably different, I wouldn't let this influence your decision.

90% of graduates currently use the internet to find jobs. Feel free to browse in job centres, newspapers and magazines but by far the most effective technique is to use the internet. There are numerous sites aimed at showcasing the latest graduate vacancies. The websites below are the most functional as they enable you to view the current graduate jobs in a particular industry. That way, once you decide what industry to work in, you can flood the whole industry with applications.

- www.graduate-jobs.co.uk
- www.milkround.co.uk
- www.doctorjob.co.uk

You may wish to post your C.V on these sites but this is unlikely to be fruitful. If you want a top job you have to make it happen. Graduate recruiters receive so many applications they have no need to chase candidates.

BLITZING THE INDUSTRY

Graduate recruiters employ strategies to reduce the number of applications they receive. This may seem counterproductive - surely the more applications, the more choice they will have. While this may be true, there is also a trade-off with time and money. Just as it is not beneficial for graduates to produce the perfect application, it is not beneficial for recruiters to try and find the perfect candidate. Sure, they would love the perfect candidate, but not at the expense it would take to find them. Techniques such as having graduate fairs only at targeted universities and adopting slogans like the Royal Marines' "99.9% need not apply" are techniques used to curtail applications. Self-assessment questionnaires on a firm's website have an analogous role. This propaganda may discourage a preacher from applying, but it should not daunt you.

Many graduates spend days determining whether or not to apply to a firm before withdrawing their application. Since you can't tell how suitable you are for the role before applying, submit applications to all jobs in the industry you choose. The only reason for not applying is if you don't meet the entry requirements. Perhaps once you start work you may find that your job is unsuitable. No problem, there are many opportunities to change track in your career and it is easier to transfer to another elite job if you have the social proof of already having been offered one. For this reason, you may wish to submit applications to a couple of industries.

STAGE 1:

ONLINE APPLICATION

OUTLINE

The online application stage comprises many or all the following sections:

- Personal details
- Education
- Work experience
- Languages
- Motivations
- Competency questions
- Extra-curricular activities
- Additional information
- Resume and cover letter

If you are lucky, the application stage will just require you to upload your resume and cover letter. Unfortunately, this is extremely rare. It is more likely you will be required to complete all the above sections.

THE OPENING SECTIONS

There is little scope for creativity in the first few sections of the online application form. The personal details, education, work experience and languages areas simply require you to fill out facts. Since players don't change provable facts, all you can do to improve your chance of success is to make sure you highlight your best aspects. For example, if you are asked to include the modules you studied at university, refrain from writing every single one down. Instead, write out the ones you did well in and feel comfortable talking about. The early sections alone will not guarantee the success of your application, but failing to meet the firms' criteria will subject your form to failure. If you want to be invited to the next stage of the application process, you will need to perform well on the subsequent sections.

CREATING STOCK ANSWERS

Since employers all seek candidates with very similar raw skills, you can be consistently successful in passing the online application stage by using stock answers and fine-tuning them to give the impression of authenticity. By creating copy and paste style answers, you can apply almost exactly the same answers to each application. This enables you to fill out a multitude of applications quickly. Creating stock answers is what the online application stage is all about. Without stock answers, the average form will take about 5 hours to complete to a successful standard. However, once you have created and saved well written answers, you can copy and paste them and complete application forms in under an hour. A regular candidate will spend weeks producing three or four applications. In the same time frame, a player will use modified stock answers to send off a vast array of applications.

Undertones of stock answers

More important than what you write, are the undertones of your answers. If you mention you go to the gym, employers will not be hiring you because you are fit - they will be impressed because going to the gym shows you are able to work on your own, you are self-motivated and you are determined. Suppose you mention you organised a sponsored cycle ride for cystic fibrosis. While your charitable nature may be an endearing feature, recruiters are more concerned with you demonstrating that the sponsored event enabled you to develop your organisational, teamwork and leadership skills. The content of the answers you produce need not be particularly impressive, but it does need to demonstrate the desirable skills the firm is pursuing.

Be professional

Producing stock responses should also improve the quality of your answers. Since you only have to write them once, you can spend time constructing well-written, professional paragraphs. You don't need to write in beautiful English as they are not looking for the next Shakespeare. However, make sure all your punctuation is correct and there are no errors. Professionalism is pertinent, as recruiters are looking for someone professional to join their firms. Nothing thrills recruiters more than seeing a form with errors because they can immediately discard it and save themselves a lot of time.

Emphasising your achievements

The quality of your stock answers is influenced by your level of honesty as well as their written professionalism. Recruiters suggest you should try and emphasise your achievements to show yourself in the best light. While this is true, the exact definition of 'emphasise' has different interpretations for everyone. Regrettably, it is those candidates who take 'emphasise' to the extreme that are most successful in the recruitment process. In a perfect world, everyone would be honest, recruiters would pick the most suitable candidates and there would be no need to misstate the truth. Unfortunately, the world of graduate recruitment is far from perfect.

THE EXTENDED QUESTIONS

To help you start, I have included my successful sample answers. I appreciate that many of my answers seem egotistical, but unfortunately, this has proven to be far more successful than being modest. The difficulty is answering the question honestly, whilst making sure your answer demonstrates the criteria they are looking for. The answers I have included will cover the majority of questions usually asked. Naturally, some forms may deviate marginally, but this is rare. It is more common that the same questions will be worded differently or asked in a different format. Rather than just copying my answers, I suggest using my answer format and tweaking it very slightly, both to your own experiences, and to the specific question you are being asked. Once you have created your own pages of stock answers, you will fly through applications.

Motivations

The first chance to use your stock answers will usually be in the motivations section – why you want to work for the company and why you have applied for the specific role. For the sake of my example we will assume you are applying to be an accountant working at company ABC. Despite recruiters looking for answers that are specific to their firm, there are certain characteristics which the majority of recruiters love to hear. Can you prove a firm has a positive working environment or an exciting graduate program? By using statements which are tricky to assign values to, you can apply stock answers to most firms by just changing the firm and job title. The lines in my stock answers below are carefully designed to reveal competencies that recruiters seek in a graduate. In the following cases, my answers demonstrate a strong work ethic, ambition, flexibility and the desire to take on responsibility from an early stage of my career. These are useful competencies to exhibit in the first section as you are rarely asked to demonstrate them later on in the application.

Why would you like to work for ABC?

ABC's prestige as a global leader, their reputation as an innovator at the forefront of business and their exciting graduate training program are all obvious motives for working for the company. However, what really attracted me to ABC was the description of the working environment referred to in numerous case-studies of current employees. While many firms offer graduate programs in accountancy, ABC appealed to me because of the challenging nature and steep learning curve that many of the employees refer to, reinforced by its positive and supportive working environment. Combining this with the opportunity to work with and be surrounded by extremely bright and talented people makes the chance to work for ABC even more attractive.

Why work as an accountant / investment banker / manager?

Following a career as an accountant has always seemed a natural extension of both my interests and my academic background. As an ambitious person I am attracted to the hard work, high risk, high reward culture offered by such a career, where I would have the opportunity to use my numeracy and analytical skills to maximize my potential. The variety of work offered is another important motive for moving into accountancy as it would enable me to gain a real insight into all aspects of the financial world.

Competencies

Whereas the above two questions are designed to be firm-specific, by virtue of the fact competency based questions require you to give examples from your past, you are able to use the same examples for different firms. This means that again, as I showed in the motivations section, you can create stock answers. These answers only need to be adjusted for different applications due to the varied wording of the questions or the word count. Don't feel that you must elongate your stock answers to use the full word count but do tailor your answers to the specific question being asked. For example, there are a million ways to ask you to demonstrate your teamwork skills and wouldn't you know it, every recruiter uses a slightly different question. Instead of rewriting a new answer for each question, you should copy and paste your teamwork example and adapt it to harmonise with the question.

The key competencies firms typically pursue include: teamwork, initiative, working under pressure, the ability to balance multiple projects, a strong work ethic, determination, being able to pursuade others and being able to overcome challenges on your own or in a team. I have included stock answers below which you can use as your own answers (providing they apply to you of course!). Alternatively, feel free to write your own answers. The list of questions below is not exhaustive, but the answers should cater for the vast majority of application forms.

Describe a time you have worked in a team.

Last year I had to perform 4 economic presentations in a group of my peers. Sometimes it was easy; everyone would be focused on our objective, we could divide tasks between ourselves, communicate well and produce an excellent group presentation. However, on a couple of occasions there were members of the group who were either too forceful or too laidback which greatly reduced the productive capacity of the group. These occasions were the most useful as they allowed us to work through the difficulties of working in a team and learn from them.

Describe a time you have demonstrated initiative.

During my second year at university I noticed that not only was everyone buying posters for their room, the posters were all of similar themes, with very few art posters either affordable or accessible. I prepared a dossier and convinced my parents to invest £300 capital to help me buy the necessary posters to establish my idea. I sold them individually on eBay, producing a return of 45% on each poster and allowing me to make a profit of over £800 in the first few months. However, as I began to sell more posters, the time taken on packaging and listing items was beginning to escalate so I set up my own website, www.anypaintings.com. Via this, people were able to view and purchase a range of art posters, with their order automatically passed on to the wholesaler to dispatch the items. This is a process called drop-shipping. Over the year of running the website I made just over £3300. In my final university year, I decided to focus on my studies and give up the business once I had made enough money to buy my first motorbike. I closed the site without regret, knowing I had the potential, ability and knowledge to set-up a profitable website if I ever felt the need or desire to do so again.

Describe a time you have worked under pressure.

Whilst working as an airside operative at Heathrow Airport, a passenger decided to get off the plane at the last minute. It was a blisteringly hot day and two others and I had just finished loading three hundred what seemed like bags of rocks. The prospect of unloading and then reloading every single bag was disheartening to say the least. It was vital we unloaded the passenger's bag in a matter of minutes otherwise the plane would miss its take-off slot. I immediately prioritised, radioed three extra people, asked the passenger for the baggage description and ticket number, phoned the check-in desk and worked out not only which baggage hold the luggage was in, but exactly where it was within the hold. We found it in under 4 minutes.

Describe a time you have overcome challenges.

The day before the rugby world cup final a friend of mine phoned me from Paris and said he had two spare world cup final tickets which I could have if I was able to get to Paris in time for the match. While arranging a trip from Leeds to Paris is normally a relatively simple task, I only had 18 hours to get there and almost every mode of transport seemed to be booked due to the massive migration of English fans.

I initially tried options such as Eurostar, P & O ferries, Norfolk ferries, Sea France etc but with no luck. I then tried flights to France from any airports in England and even looked at booking flights to other destinations in Europe and getting the train to Paris but all were booked. To overcome the problem and since time was of the essence I contacted about 15 of my friends who helped with the search process using the internet, phones and any sources of information possible. I had a couple of friends who have websites so I got them to write posts on them requesting information on anyone with tickets to France. However, nobody replied.

After a couple of hours, one of my friends finally found an Australian who had booked coach tickets from London to Paris, presuming Australia would get to the final. She was more than happy to sell her tickets so a friend and I travelled through the night to London to pick-up the tickets... then on to the world cup final in Paris!

Describe a time you have overcome challenges when working in a team.

Whilst in the 6th form my friends and I raised £545 for my local football team on a sponsored cycle ride round Yorkshire. As well as planning the routes, we arranged publicity and secured business sponsorship. We achieved this by phoning and writing to local companies, approaching business associations and negotiating publicity with a local radio station. However, torrential rain throughout caused us to change our plan. Initially, we had decided that we should sleep in tents to save money but after 3 days of torrential rain, every campsite we came across was too waterlogged to stay at. Consequently, our only alternative was to try and stay in local bed and breakfasts or hotels.

Rather than spend money on this, we managed to convince 3 hotels over the final 3 days of our trip to give us free accommodation in return for publicity, allowing us to contribute the money saved to the total sponsorship raised.

Describe a time you have had to persuade others to overcome resistance.

Whilst working as Assistant Manager at Henley House I noticed that everyone entering Henley House bird garden was queuing round the back of the cafe. I suggested moving the entrance so all visitors were channelled through the courtyard section of the café. When I approached my boss with this idea he was initially against the idea due to the £14,000 costs. I decided to set-up a simple survey and got £400 from my boss to fund the questionnaire. The results convinced my boss that the project was financially viable and so he gave the go ahead. Turnover in the first month after installation of the new entrance increased by 32% meaning the installation costs were offset in well under a year.

Describe a time when you have had to juggle many projects at one time.

During my final year of university I managed a job working two nights a week, my economics work and my numerous extra-curricular activities. As well as being captain and top goal scorer two years running for both my university football teams, I am opening batsman and wicketkeeper for my cricket club and regularly compete in both squash and snooker tournaments. I am also a keen member of the university boxing club and took part in last year's prestigious BUSA tournament.

Outside sport I am a Karnival representative for my university hall. I organise weekly buses and supervise first year students, visiting cities around the country collecting money for charity. Nottingham University Karnival is the largest student run charitable organisation in the country, with a turnover of over £500,000 a year.

Whilst it takes both self-motivation and self-discipline to take part in so many extra-curricular activities, it has also helped improve my organisational skills, allowing me to follow my love for sport without compromising my studies. Recently, I have not only had to meet job application deadlines but also deadlines for two large pieces of economics coursework. Despite it not being easy to manage everything at once, I have maintained a high standard of work by being well organised and prioritising my most important tasks. Consequently, my economics work has not been jeopridised.

Extra-curricular activites

This section requires you to look like a well rounded individual whilst at the same time demonstrating the traits the recruiter is seeking in a candidate. Sporting achievements are a good example as they require many of the skills crucial to being a success in the world of work such as self motivation and discipline, whilst at the same time showing you have more to offer than just an academic background. If you are not sporting, other activities such as joining organisations, clubs or societies are just as good. If you really don't have time or you prefer not to join clubs, maybe you could join a few for a week. That way they can be included without you lying.

Describe your major achievements or extra-curricular activities you partake in.

The wide array of sports facilities available at university has enabled me to develop my passion for sport. As well as being captain and top goal scorer two years running for both my university football teams, I was a keen member of the university boxing club and won both my hall squash and snooker tournaments. Whilst it takes both self-motivation and self-discipline to take part in so many extra-curricular activities, it has also helped improve my organisational skills, allowing me to follow my love for sport without compromising my studies. Through sport I have learnt both to lead as a captain and work in a team striving to reach a common goal.

Whilst in the 6th form, I raised £515 for my local football team by persuading 4 friends to join me in a sponsored cycle round Yorkshire. As well as planning the routes, I arranged publicity and secured business sponsorship. I achieved this by phoning and writing to local companies, approaching business associations and negotiating publicity with a local radio station. When torrential rain threatened the event, I convinced local hotels to give us free accommodation in return for publicity.

Academically, I have received several rewards including the Julia Wiltshire Memorial prize for Economics, Prince Edward's Certificate of Merit for Outstanding Performance and the Business Dynamics Certificate of Achievement

Aditional Information

There may be an additional information section which is usually optional. It is wise to fill this in if you feel the questions on the application form have not enabled you to highlight why you are an outstanding candidate for the job. Again, I have a stock answer which I copied and pasted into each application form. If I had already given examples demonstrating the competencies below, I would just include examples of alternative competencies specific to the role. I do suggest writing an additional information section because almost every application form offers a dedicated space and it only takes a second to paste in.

What additional information would support your application?

I believe my academic background and specifically my university course have enabled me to develop both an analytical mind and clarity of expression. However the more I read on both accountancy and ABC, the more clear it became that while these skills were a solid foundation; to be successful in accountancy, they must be complemented by interpersonal skills, teamwork and the ability to work under pressure.

Interpersonal skills - I developed my interpersonal skills over the two years I worked as Assistant manager at Henley House café, managing staff and addressing customer queries and complaints. I learnt the importance of really listening to people's concerns, showing them respect, understanding their point of view and being diplomatic enough to help them find a satisfactory solution. I spent this summer further enhancing this skill by working as a barman as I believed this transferable skill would be particularly useful in accountancy.

Teamwork - Last year I had to give 4 economics presentations in a group with six peers enabling me to enhance the teamwork skills that I had developed from being a member of so many sports teams. I learnt a lot about negotiating points of view and reaching consensus through reasoned discussion.

Working under pressure - As a baggage handler I had to unload a specific bag from a fully loaded plane in a matter of minutes otherwise the plane would miss its take-off slot. I immediately prioritized, radioed a couple of extra people to help, asked the passenger for the baggage description and ticket number, phoned the check-in desk and worked not only which baggage hold the luggage was in, but exactly where it was within the hold. We found it in less than 4 minutes.

C.V & COVER LETTER

To create a successful C.V and covering letter quickly, don't waste time reading numerous books on creating the 'perfect C.V'. A perfect CV is described differently by everyone so should not be sought. Unfortunately, this only became apparent to me after wasting weeks reading three mind numbingly dull books on the subject. The application process has however enlightened me with the knowledge that there are C.V and cover letters that consistently interest recruiters enough to invite you to the next stage of the process. Luckily for you, I have included mine, or at least a C.V and cover letter very similar to mine (with a few details changed for 'legal reasons'!).

You may read them and be distinctly unimpressed. Perhaps you think they are too simple or too short. Like every aspect of the application process, nothing the player submits is done by mistake. If it looks short, it is because short has provided the best results. If the Garamond font looks a touch medieval, it is because a touch medieval works best.

To be successful, you should use this C.V and cover letter as templates. There is a strong probability you could write superior alternatives, but why take the chance when these two are proven to work consistently? The more deviations you make, the more risks you are taking. If I were you, I would use the exact same format in both, just changing the content where necessary.

If you must deviate from the C.V format, there are certain points you should remember:

- The best C.V is concise, so exclude any point that doesn't add anything. It should be no longer than two pages - preferably one.
- Make it clear and arrange the information in a logical order.
- Look for gaps in your C.V and either fill them or come up with impressive reasons to account for them
- Try and tailor the information to the industry you are applying for.

If you must deviate from the cover letter format, there are certain points you should remember:

- Make sure it fits onto one side of A4.
- Use persuasive language to convince the recruiter to meet you.
- Spend time producing thoughtful, succinct sentences.
- Try and relate your information to the industry you are applying for.

BOBBY DACRE

EDUCATION

2004-2007 BA (Hons) Economics at Leeds University - 2:1

1995-2002 Prince Edward's Grammar School
Head Boy and Form Representative for three years

2002 A in A-level English
      B in A-level French
      C in A-level German
2001 D in AS Russian
2000 10 GCSEs (3As, 4Bs, 3Cs)

ACADEMIC HONOURS

Julie Wiltshire Memorial prize for Economics

Prince Edward's Certificate of Merit for Outstanding Performance

Business Dynamics Certificate of Achievement

INTERESTS

As well as being captain and top goal scorer two years running for both my university football teams, I was opening batsman and wicketkeeper for my cricket club and won both my hall squash and snooker tournaments. I am also a keen member of the university boxing and tennis clubs.

WORK EXPERIENCE

2006-2007 Lifeguard – Leeds International Pool

2006 Barman – The Happy Return Public House

2005 Airside Operative – Heathrow Airport

2000-2002 Assistant Manager - Henley House Café

2000 Office Junior – Morris & Son solicitors

VOLUNTEER WORK

2005 University Karni Representative

2004 Hall Sports Secretary

2000 -2001 School Football Team Manager

05/01/08

Dear Sir / Madam

I am writing to apply for your accountancy graduate scheme and enclose my C.V for your kind attention. I was particularly attracted to ABC because of the high standing of the company within the industry and the excellence of the graduate programme, enabling graduates to take on great responsibility from an early stage in their career.

Following a career in accountancy seems a natural extension of both my interests and academic background. ABC provides an exciting opportunity to learn all the financial aspects of business, work with talented, hardworking individuals and build a network of well-connected professionals. As an ambitious person I am attracted to the hard work, high risk, high reward culture offered by such a career, where I would have the opportunity to maximise my potential.

I completed my Economics (Hons) degree from the University of Leeds in June and will be available to begin employment from July. Studying economics was particularly beneficial as the course combines both highly complex mathematical concepts with the requirement of producing clear, well structured, eloquent essay answers. Additionally, I was required to work both in teams performing presentations and on my own. Due to the low number of lectures and lack of guidance, I gained the ability to take the initiative, to see what tasks need carrying out and to complete them with minimal supervision. Combining these skills with interpersonal skills enhanced from working as Assistant Manager at Henley House, teamwork skills gained from playing in numerous sports teams and the ability to work accurately under pressure accrued from working at Heathrow Airport provide an excellent foundation on which to build a successful career with ABC.

Outside work I am a passionate sportsman and lifelong Leeds United supporter (an example of loyalty if ever there was one!) and would welcome the opportunity to bring this same passion and loyalty to my work. I like to work hard and play hard; going the extra mile to deliver excellence and believe this would match the ethos of your company. I would be very grateful for the chance to show you what I can do.

Thank you for your consideration.

Yours truly,

Bobby Dacre

STAGE 2:

PSYCHOMETRIC TESTING

OUTLINE

Typically the electrifying process that is psychometric testing will take place once your online application is successful. Sometimes they will save these tests to the assessment day or even after, but most commonly you are invited to take the online tests in stage 2. Over 85% of employers now use psychometric testing. These tests include:

- Numerical test
- Verbal test
- Personality questionnaire

Put simply, there is a maths test, a comprehension test and a survey to check your personality complements their company culture. It is conceivable they might include a variance of these tests. However, as previously mentioned, we players do not waste our time learning things that have a very negligible chance of being in the application process. I have been bombarded with tests in my time and only once have I encountered an alternative style of test. Psychometric tests are designed to test your natural ability - your raw skills. The good news is that they do not. With just a few hours practice you can improve your scores considerably.

I have spent more time than I care to remember, writing 50 numerical and 50 verbal questions to help you practice. These have been divided equally into two verbal and two numerical tests. If you were to take them under exam conditions, aim to complete each numerical test in 25 minutes and each verbal test in 20 minutes. The questions I have written have been carefully designed to cover the full range of common questions you will encounter. You should endeavour to get 70% in each test. Don't worry if when you start you only get 30% - with practice you will dramatically increase your score. Also, don't be concerned if you fail to complete the tests in the required time. With practice you will increase your speed. Some firms are more concerned with accuracy and others with the aggregation of your correct scores. As a player you should be concerned with both. If you are running out of time at the end of the test and have to choose, I would remain accurate and refrain from guessing the remaining questions.

Combining the 100 questions in this book with the SHL practice papers should guarantee that you have enough practice before attempting real psychometric tests. Master these questions and you are effectively guaranteed to pass the psychometric test stage. If you require extra practice, check out the ASE and Kent websites below. Be warned - these websites use questions of a less commonly used format so are less relevant:

- www.shl.com
- www.ase-solutions.co.uk
- www.kent.ac.uk/careers/tests

NUMERICAL TEST

One of the graduate psychometric books I read suggested training your mind to improve your numerical test scores by going on a run each morning and adding up the numbers on the car registration plates. Then, when you improve you should practice multiplying the numbers! This is just another example of someone who has never done psychometric tests coming up with some 'revolutionary, performance enhancing' technique. A player does not adhere to recruiters' pathetic ideas. We follow techniques that produce results. If you can answer all the questions below, you will be able to pass the vast majority of numerical tests recruiters can throw at you – providing you don't panic or make too many mistakes. You don't need to get full marks; in fact 60% should be sufficient to pass many tests. However, it is advisable to learn how to do the following questions expertly, just in case you make mistakes in your test or in the unlikely event that recruiters ask you some alternative questions.

Test 1

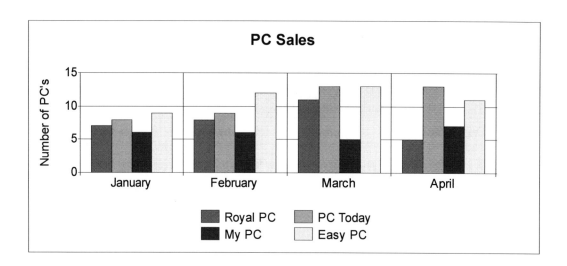

1) Which month showed the greatest total fall in PC sales over the previous month?

a) January

b) February

c) March

d) Cannot say

2) Approximately what percentage of Royal PC's sales was in April?

a) 16%

b) 17%

c) 18%

d) 31%

3) If over all four months the average profit made on each PC sold by PC Today was £75, what was the total profit over the four months for this shop?

a) £3115

b) £3225

c) £3335

d) £3445

Cost of Item (£)	Shop A	Shop B
0 – 0.99	12%	15%
1 – 4.99	24%	29%
5 – 19.99	21%	25%
20 – 99.99	21%	18%
100 – 999.99	12%	7%
1000 +	10%	6%
Total Items	14,800	11,600

4) If the quantity of items less than £5 increased by 10% per year at Shop A and 5 % per year at Shop B, what would be the approximate difference between the number of items on sale for under £5 after 4 years?

a) 1595

b) 1244

c) 84

d) Cannot say

5) What percentage of the items on sale in both shops is cheaper than £20?

a) 62.3%

b) 63.3%

c) 64.3%

d) 65.3%

6) If Shop A were to raise the cost of all items by 50p, what percentage of items would cost less than £5?

a) 36%

b) 41%

c) 46%

d) Cannot say

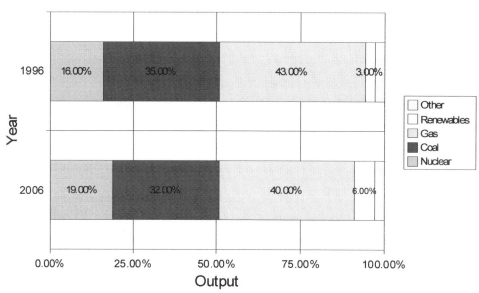

7) What percentage of 2006 output was not from Renewable, Gas, Coal or Nuclear energy production?

a) 1%

b) 3%

c) 5

d) 7%

8) If 2006 output for Nuclear was double that for 1996 Coal when total output was 200TWh, what was the output for Gas in 2006?

a) 140 TWh

b) 145 TWh

c) 295 TWh

d) 305 TWh

9) If total output was 200TWh in 1996 and 320TWh in 2006, what was the total output in 2000?

a) 241 TWh

b) 243 TWh

c) 249 TWh

d) Cannot say

Reason for Refund	% This Year	% Last Year
Faulty Software	21	23
Faulty Hardware	27	21
Damage during Delivery	11	7
Poor Customer Service	23	28
False Advertisement	8	12
Other	10	9

10) Total refunds increased by 20% from last years total of 456. Approximately, what number of refunds was issued this year due to Delivery Damage?

a) 60

b) 70

c) 80

d) 90

11) If refunds last year totalled 400 and there had been a 15% increase in the number of refunds due to faulty hardware from the year before, approximately what number of complaints was received in this category 2 years ago?

a) 71

b) 72

c) 142

d) 144

12) If refunds totalled 905 last year and 705 this year, what was the percentage fall in faulty hardware?

a) 7%

b) 12%

c) 19%

d) No change

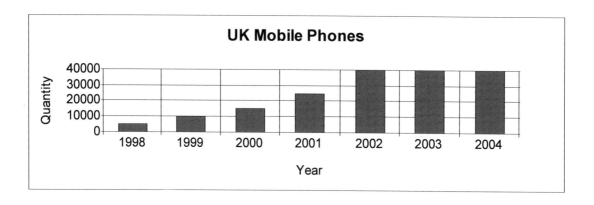

Market Share in 2004					
Nokia	Motorola	Siemens	Samsung	Ericsson	Others
32%	17%	14%	12%	9%	16%

13) How many Motorola users were there in 2004?
a) 6,800

b) 7,000

c) 7,200

d) 7,400

14) If Siemens market share was 19% in 1999, how does the number of Siemens users in 1999 compare to that of 2004?

a) 3,700 less

b) 3,700 more

c) 4,700 less

d) 4,700 more

15) In 2004, how many extra mobile phone users would Ericsson require to be on a par with Nokia?

a) 3,600

b) 9,200

c) 12,800

d) 15,600

	2002	2003	2004
Number of Graduates	1600	1650	1700
Percent in employment	42	46	31
Percent studying	41	36	35
Percent unemployed	15	16	28
Percent other	2	2	6

16) What was the highest number of students in any year that continued studying?

a) 594

b) 656

c) 672

d) 681

17) What was the fall in the number of graduates in employment between 2002 and 2004?

a) 140

b) 145

c) 150

d) 155

18) If in 2003 the percentage of social science students was 34%, approximately what was the number of social science students in employment after graduating that year?

a) 108

b) 158

c) 208

d) 258

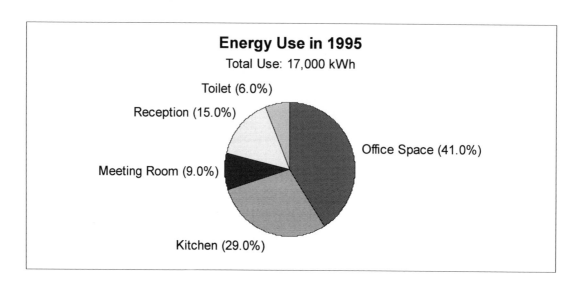

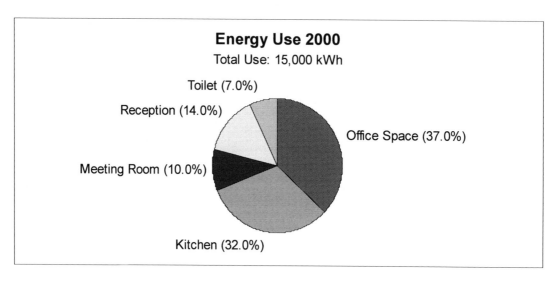

19) Between 1995 and 2000, what was the reduction in energy use for the Reception, Meeting Rooms and Office Space combined?

a) 1,900 kWh

b) 3,150 kWh

c) 10,150 kWh

d) 11,050 kWh

20) If the total energy usage today is 6% less than it was in 2000, by how much has today's usage fallen in comparison to 1995?

a) 17.06%

b) 17.08%

c) 17.10%

d) 17.12%

21) Which room incurred the smallest change in energy use between 1995 and 2000?

a) Toilet

b) Reception

c) Kitchen

d) Office Space

Population Structure 1990					
	Pop at start of year (mil)	Births per 1000 pop (Jan –Dec)	Deaths per 1000 pop (Jan –Dec)	Percentage of population at start of year aged	
				Under 15	60 or over
UK	58.9	13.9	11.3	18	21
France	57.8	14.2	10.7	17	21
Australia	48.8	8.1	6.7	19	26
Germany	87.8	8.2	11,9	12	27
Italy	54.8	13.7	7.9	21	16

22) How many live births occurred in 1990 in Italy and Australia combined?
a) 1,146,040

b) 1,246,040

c) 1,346,040

d) Cannot say

23) Which country had the highest number of people younger than 15 at the start of 1990?
a) Germany

b) Italy

c) France

d) U.K

24) What was the net effect on the UK population of the birth and death rates in 1990?
a) 134,230 decrease

b) 134,230 increase

c) 153,140 decrease

d) 153,140 increase

25) What percentage of the French population were aged 60 or over at the end of 1990?
a) 22%

b) 32%

c) 42%

d) Cannot say

Test 2

Company	Annual Profit (£)	Cost to Buy (£)	No. of Employees
Top Male	22,000	17,000	5
The Head Shop	27,000	26,000	11
Come Meet	19,000	22,000	10
Dickson's	33,000	32,000	14

26) Which company has the greatest annual profit per employee?

a) Top Male

b) The Head Shop

c) Come Meet

d) Dickson's

27) If the profits per employee remained constant, how many extra employees would Dickson's have to recruit to attain annual profits of £39,000?

a) 3

b) 4

c) 5

d) 6

28) If an investor acquired The Head Shop and the profits for each company remained constant, how much money would the investor have made after two years?

a) £2,700

b) £2,800

c) £27,000

d) £28,000

Town		Jan	Feb	Mar	Apr	Average cost per accident (£)
Otley	Accidents	12	11	8	19	1,750
	Vehicles on road (000's)	54	59	49	69	
Yeadon	Accidents	19	19	16	21	2,755
	Vehicles on road (000's)	87	85	81	91	
Harrogate	Accidents	25	29	27	32	1,265
	Vehicles on road (000's)	122	121	125	132	

29) What was the average accident cost per vehicle on the road in Otley during January?

a) £0.36

b) £0.37

c) £0.38

d) £0.39

30) What was the difference in average accident cost per vehicle on the road in February between Yeadon and Harrogate?

a) £0.29

b) £0.32

c) £0.38

d) £0.39

31) What was the average accident cost per vehicle in all the towns in March?

a) £0.36

b) £0.39

c) £0.42

d) £0.45

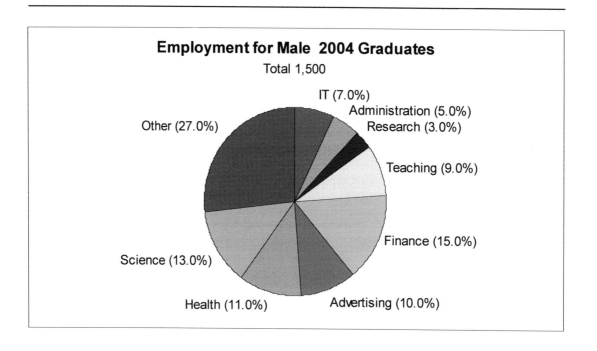

Employment for Male 2004 Graduates
Total 1,500

IT (7.0%)
Administration (5.0%)
Research (3.0%)
Other (27.0%)
Teaching (9.0%)
Finance (15.0%)
Science (13.0%)
Health (11.0%)
Advertising (10.0%)

32) 31% of male graduates enrol in:
a) IT, Administration & Science

b) Administration, Research & Other

c) Teaching, Finance, Advertising

d) IT, Teaching & Finance

33) How many extra males went into Health than Teaching?
a) 30

b) 32

c) 34

d) 36

34) If the number of males in finance increased by 7% for the next 3 years, how many more males would there be in Science and Health combined (assuming their numbers stay constant)?
a) 65

b) 75

c) 85

d) 95

	Time to manufacture (seconds)		
	Small (S)	Medium (M)	Large (L)
T-Shirt	320	320	320
Jumper	360	360	360
Untailored Shirt	360	380	400
Jacket	760	800	840

35) To manufacture a Tailored Shirt takes four and a half times as long as it does to manufacture an Untailored Shirt. How many more Untailored (L) than Tailored (L) shirts can be manufactured in 10 hours?
a) 60

b) 65

c) 70

d) 75

36) Each T-Shirt generates £1.55 profit and each Jumper £1.85. What is the difference in profit produced per hour between T-shirts and Jumpers?

a) £1.07

b) £1.14

c) £1.21

d) £1.28

37) How many more entire Jackets (S) than Jackets (L) can be manufactured in a fourteen hour shift?

a) 5

b) 6

c) 7

d) 8

Industry	Male	Female
Charity	25,000	27,000
IT	128,000	67,000
Legal	118,000	125,000
Health	164,000	223,000
Engineering	156,000	101,000
Unemployed	63,000	68,000
Total	654,000	611,000

38) Approximately, what proportion of the people tested is unemployed?
a) 10.4%

b) 10.1%

c) 9.4%

d) 9.1%

39) If the quantity of females working in Health increases by 10% per year, but the quantity of males remains constant, what percentage of Health employees would be female in three years?
a) 44.4%

b) 54.4%

c) 64.4%

d) 74.4%

40) What ratio of males to females is unemployed?
a) 2:3

b) 3:5

c) 4:9

d) 126:136

	UK Pound (June 2000)	US Dollar (June 2000)
UK Pound	1.00	1.89
US Dollar	0.53	1.00
Canadian Dollar	0.50	0.94
Euro	0.66	1.24
Russian Roubles	0.020	0.038

41) Approximately, how many UK Pounds was 200 U.S dollars worth in 2000?
a) £53

b) £106

c) £530

d) £1060

42) Approximately, how many Euros was 55 Russian Roubles worth in June 2000?
a) 1.63

b) 1.67

c) 1.73

d) 1.77

43) Approximately, how many extra Canadian Dollars would you get if you swapped 350 UK Pounds rather than 200 US Dollars?
a) 478

b) 488

c) 498

d) 508

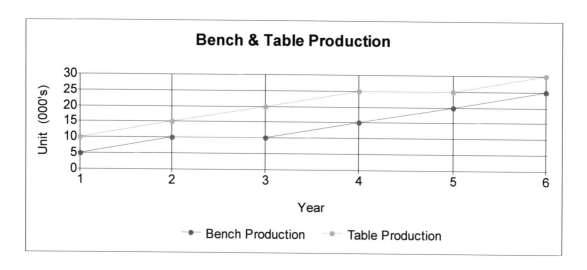

44) What was the difference in combined bench and table production in year five and year six?

a) 20

b) 20,000

c) 10,000

d) No change

45) Suppose total production costs in year 3 were £150,000. If it costs £2.50 to produce one table, how much did it cost to produce one bench?

a) £5
b) £9
c) £10
d) Cannot say

46) Over the six year period, what percentage of total production did benches account for?

a) 39.5%

b) 40.0%

c) 40.5%

d) 41.0%

Mass (Kg)	UK Number of Cars (000's)		Italy Number of Cars (000's)	
	1998	**2003**	**1998**	**2003**
0-499	5	9	4	12
500-999	24	32	59	99
1000-1499	283	386	354	465
1500-1999	402	498	512	598
2000+	65	34	67	23

47) How many cars under 2,000kg were there in Italy in 1998?
a) 899,000

b) 909,000

c) 919,000

d) 929,000

48) What was the total mass of all the cars in the UK in 2003?
a) 258,000kg

b) 1,258,000kg

c) 12,580,000kg

d) Cannot say

49) In the UK, what was the percentage increase in the total number of cars between 1998 and 2003?
a) 21.1%

b) 22.1%

c) 23.1%

d) 24.1%

50) How many cars will there be with a mass of under 500kg in 2005 if the total mass of cars declines by 5% from the 2003 levels?
a) 8,550

b) 9,450

c) 9,950

d) Cannot say

Answers

1	d) Cannot say	26	a) Top Male
2	a) 16%	27	a) 3
3	b) 3,225	28	d) £28,000
4	a) 1,595	29	d) £0.39
5	a) 62.3%	30	b) £0.32
6	d) Cannot say	31	a) £0.36
7	b) 3%	32	d) IT, Teach & Finance
8	c) 295 TWh	33	a) 30
9	d) Cannot say	34	c) 85
10	a) 60	35	c) 70
11	a) 71	36	a) £1.07
12	d) No change	37	b) 6
13	a) 6,800	38	a) 10.4%
14	a) 3700 less	39	c) 64.4%
15	b) 9,200	40	d) 126:136
16	b) 656	41	b) £106
17	b) 145	42	b) €1.67
18	d) 258	43	b) 488
19	a) 1,900 kWh	44	c) 10,000
20	a) 17.06%	45	c) £10
21	b) Reception	46	c) 40.5%
22	a) 1,146,040	47	d) 929,000
23	b) Italy	48	d) Cannot say
24	d) 153,140 +	49	c) 23.1%
25	d) Cannot say	50	d) Cannot say

VERBAL TESTS

Unlike numerical tests, verbal tests are relatively subjective. The idea is to decide whether a statement is true or false based only on the information in the article, or the information you can infer from the article. It is the "infer" part which makes this section tricky. After all, what you can infer from a passage is highly subjective. It is important that you only look at the article and refrain from using your own knowledge to form conclusions. For this reason I advise caution when answering questions on articles covering content you are familiar with since you will subconsciously apply your own understanding to bias your answers. If the article doesn't prove the statement true or false and neither answer can be inferred, you should answer "cannot say". As you will see from the answer sheet, "cannot say" is the correct answer surprisingly frequently so don't feel like you are failing by using it. The best way to excel at verbal questions is to practice comprehension and gain an understanding of what is deemed inferable. To master this section, specifically practice these and the SHL questions.

Credit card fraud has increased to an all time high despite the introduction of new controls. A recent report showed that losses to fraud rose by 20 per cent last year alone. The majority of credit card frauds result from cards intercepted in the post. The banks knew the year would be problematic as it was thought that fraudsters would try to commit as many crimes as possible before new controls were introduced. It is believed that in a years time the effect of the new measures will be known and the level of fraud will have dropped significantly.

1) Credit card fraud from cards stolen in the post is the most common type of fraud.

A) True   B) Not True   C) Cannot say

2) New anti-fraud measures are highly sophisticated.

A) True   B) Not True   C) Cannot say

3) The new measures are now fully in place.

A) True   B) Not True   C) Cannot say

For 18 successive years the A-level pass rate has improved. It is not the case that exam questions have got easier, rather, students find it easier to gain top grades now that marks are awarded for course and project work. Only 20% of the marks are reserved for the final exams. Last year

140,000 girls obtained two A grades whereas 18 years ago only 38,000 obtained these grades. Before 1990, grades were norm-rated against previous years, with only a tenth of candidates being awarded A grades. There is now no limit on the number of A grades so anyone who scores over 60% receives an A grade. Consequently, the number of A grades awarded has more than doubled.

4) Top grades are more easily attainable due to the examining method.

A) True   B) Not True   C) Cannot say

5) The rise in the number of A grades is mainly due to girls.

A) True   B) Not True   C) Cannot say

6) 20% of pupils get a score of over 60%.

A) True   B) Not True   C) Cannot say

Contingent valuation rose to prominence in the 1980s, chiefly in environmental economics as an instrument for measuring the economic valuation of environmental projects and damage assessment after environmental accidents. Recently, a large number of contingent valuation studies have arisen in the health care field, valuating a spread of diseases and treatments including cystic fibrosis and anti-depressants. The fact that the contingent valuation is built on asking people questions, rather than analysing individuals' actions has caused great scepticism due to the conceptual, empirical and practical problems associated with assigning monetary estimates of economic value on the basis of how surveyed individuals respond to hypothetical questions.

7) Contingent valuation assigns monetary valuations based the predictions of economists.

A) True   B) Not True   C) Cannot say

8) Contingent valuation rose to prominence as an instrument for forecasting the costs of environmental projects and accidents.

A) True   B) Not True   C) Cannot say

9) Contingent valuation is revolutionising the health care field.

A) True   B) Not True   C) Cannot say

Medicine has traditionally been the science of curing illness. For thousands of years people used natural remedies and turned to priests for cures. Recently, illness has been attributed to natural causes rather than the intervention of gods. Medicine today is just as concerned with prevention as cure. Doctors use a range of treatments including recent types such as vaccination and radiation, as well as treatments practiced for centuries. Europeans have adopted many of the treatments used for centuries in North and South America and some are still effective and in use today.

10) Modern medicine is only concerned with curing illness.

A) True   B) Not True   C) Cannot say

11) Medicine owes its success to modern techniques and treatments.

A) True   B) Not True   C) Cannot say

12) Vaccination is a fairly new discovery.

A) True   B) Not True   C) Cannot say

Since nuclear power stations are carbon-free, building them would address the long-term environmental problem of carbon emissions. However, even though new power plants produce smaller amounts of radioactive waste than older ones, there is still the problem of radioactive waste. Additionally, nuclear power's electricity is more expensive than that of carbon-producing plants such as coal. Conversely, renewable energy sources are comparatively cheap and have the potential to become even cheaper. Their major drawback is the visual intrusion they cause, but this is reversible and can be limited by appropriate planning.

13) If the problem of radioactive waste could be resolved there would be a good environmental case for nuclear power.

A) True   B) Not True   C) Cannot say

14) Carbon-free alternatives to nuclear power also have problems.

A) True   B) Not True   C) Cannot say

15) Renewable power sources are carbon free.

A) True   B) Not True   C) Cannot say

While education in developing countries is crucial in enhancing worker productivity and enabling long term economic growth, widespread emigration of the most educated means the costs of education are borne by the developing country without future productivity gains. Additionally, the loss of the most educated workers means the loss of future leaders, physicians, teachers and other professionals leaving huge occupational gaps which developing countries are unable to fill. The vast sacrifices made by developing countries to educate workers to a high level reap few rewards as the developed countries gain the dividends "The emigration of African professionals to the West is one of the greatest obstacles to Africa's development." (United Nations Economic Commission for Africa).

16) Emigration is having a nominal affect on Africa.

A) True   B) Not True   C) Cannot say

17) The donor country pays the costs of educating its emigrating workers.

A) True   B) Not True   C) Cannot say

18) Only educated workers emigrate from developing countries.

A) True   B) Not True   C) Cannot say

Persuading people to favour bus travel over their car is tricky. Governments have attempted to achieve this goal by improving comfort and frequency of public transport. However, this has minimal effects as people value their cars too highly. The opposition from the general public to governmental persuasion has already been demonstrated during the petrol blockade. The most probable solutions are ones that retain the most driver convenience, whilst keeping costs low. One popular suggestion is to improve public transport so cars are needed less. This can be gradually implemented and has the benefit of using existing road systems.

19) The view of the government is that improving the comfort of buses will encourage people to use them.

A) True   B) Not True   C) Cannot say

20) In the past, the actions of government have led to a petrol blockade.

A) True   B) Not True   C) Cannot say

21) If buses were cheaper and ran more frequently, more people would use them.

A) True   B) Not True   C) Cannot say

The latest changes to the postal voting system are deemed by election officials to notably increase the threat of electoral fraud. If it were to be prevalent, such fraud could discredit the entire electoral process. The majority of concerns centre around the very limited time the new system allows electoral administrators to verify that requests for postal ballots are authentic. The government is eager to increase the quantity of people who cast a vote and believe that people should not be deprived of a vote simply because they do not apply in good time. Fraud at this time is rare and there is so far no evidence of postal votes causing widespread fraud.

22) The government has been informed by electoral officials that risk of fraud is now higher.

A) True   B) Not True   C) Cannot say

23) The present level of fraud is too insignificant to bring the electoral system into disrepute.

A) True   B) Not True   C) Cannot say

24) The previous postal system was thought by election administrators to be less susceptible to fraud.

A) True   B) Not True   C) Cannot say

25) There is a procedure for checking the validity of postal vote applications.

A) True   B) Not True   C) Cannot say

Test 2

Conventional currency crisis models focus primarily on the exchange rate. The first crisis models, the canonical models suggest that a government with persistent money-financed budget deficits is assumed to use a limited stock of reserves to peg its exchange rate. In the long-run this policy is unsustainable as the attempts of investors to anticipate the unavoidable downfall would generate a speculative attack on the currency when reserves fell to some critical level. In subsequent currency crisis models, policy is less mechanical. A government chooses whether or not to defend

the pegged exchange rate by choosing between short-run macroeconomic flexibility and longer-term credibility. If the market believes that defending the parity will fail, defence is more expensive as higher interest rates will be required. Consequently, a speculative attack on a currency can develop either as a result of a predicted future decline in fundamentals, or merely through self-fulfilling prophecy.

26) Canonical models suggest a currency crisis is more probable in a country with low reserves.

A) True   B) Not True   C) Cannot say

27) Defending a currency is more expensive than not, as higher interest rates are required.

A) True   B) Not True   C) Cannot say

28) There is nothing a government can do to avoid speculative attacks as they are a self-fulfilling prophecy.

A) True   B) Not True   C) Cannot say

Crude oil levels are monitored by traders to establish the markets' long term natural supply and demand levels. Hoarding was a major contributor to high crude oil prices in the 1970s and evidence is again suggesting that hoarding is causing current record high crude prices. Crude stocks fell because refiners had adopted just-in-time stock management policies. However, the purchasing of oil at levels well above their rate of consumption by some countries suggests that the hoarding of oil stocks is once again occurring. The increased recent consumption by developing nations such as China and India has led traders to revise upwards their levels of natural global demand for crude oil.

29) The idea that current high crude prices are being supported by the hoarding of stock is factually unsupported.

A) True   B) Not True   C) Cannot say

30) If we assume hoarding is supporting high prices then prices will fall back once hoards have been established.

A) True   B) Not True   C) Cannot say

31) China and India recently became major oil importers.

A) True   B) Not True   C) Cannot say

The brain is the control centre of the body. It is composed of billions of neurons. It keeps the body working and is also responsible for your thoughts, feelings and memory. Different parts of the brain have different functions; for example the medulla oblongata controls involuntary activities such as breathing and heart rate. The largest area of the brain is the cerebrum which controls conscious feelings and voluntary movements. It is also responsible for intelligence and learning.

32) The medulla oblongata controls all subconscious activities.

A) True   B) Not True   C) Cannot say

33) The brain controls how we feel.

A) True   B) Not True   C) Cannot say

34) More intelligent people have larger cerebrums.

A) True   B) Not True   C) Cannot say

The aim of the GCH centre is a 25% reduction in carbon dioxide emissions by 2010. A report showed that improving energy efficiency in buildings is the cheapest option to achieve this target. Without mandatory policies in place, it is the responsibility of centre managers to lead by example. The best solution is to use a combined heat and power unit to increase energy efficiency. This would satisfy the heating demand for both the domestic hot water system and the swimming pool, but would not be appropriate for space heating requirements.

35) Improving the energy efficiency of buildings is the only way to meet the emissions target.

A) True   B) Not True   C) Cannot say

36) Legal obligations are the reason the centre is looking to improve efficiency

A) True   B) Not True   C) Cannot say

37) The heating requirements for the full building cannot be satisfied by the combined heat and power unit alone.

A) True   B) Not True   C) Cannot say

The relationship between demographics and savings is sometimes based on the theory that young people borrow, middle-aged people save and the elderly draw from their savings. Therefore, borrowing will be highest when a population is disproportionately young, and savings should peak when that disproportional cohort reaches middle age.

38) It is reasonable to assume that the cost of borrowing will be high and the yield from savings will be low when the population is disproportionately young.

A) True   B) Not True   C) Cannot say

39) According to this theory, a high level of savings can only be brought about by a proportionately middle-aged population.

A) True   B) Not True   C) Cannot say

40) A predominantly middle-aged population will have a lower cost of borrowing than a predominantly old-aged population.

A) True   B) Not True   C) Cannot say

Light is made up of packets of energy called photons. Some photons have more energy than others. Light can be thought of as a wave which has different wavelengths with different types of photon. Light with a short wavelength has high-energy photons. Light with a long wavelength has low-energy photons. Only certain wavelengths of light are visible to the human eye. This range of wavelengths is called the visible spectrum and contains light that is coloured.

41) There are certain wavelengths of light in the visual spectrum that humans cannot see.

A) True   B) Not True   C) Cannot say

42) Photons are packets of energy involved in hearing.

A) True   B) Not True   C) Cannot say

43) There is a correlation between the wavelength of light and the energy of the photons.

A) True   B) Not True   C) Cannot say

When a customer uses their phone abroad, charges known as roaming charges are levied by network service providers. There are reports stating that the UK is paying an inflated rate, especially considering that customers in Germany, Belgium, Sweden and Holland are paying less for the equivalent service. There is a lack of understanding by many customers of the roaming charges which sometimes apply even for receiving calls while abroad. Better consumer information is necessary if there is to be an equalisation of pre-pay international roaming charges in the UK and the rest of Europe.

44) It is cheaper for UK customers to use a roaming service than it is for Swedish customers.

A) True   B) Not True   C) Cannot say

45) Pre-pay roaming rates are mainly cheaper than pay-as-you-go rates.

A) True   B) Not True   C) Cannot say

46) Customers are never charged for calls they do not make.

A) True   B) Not True   C) Cannot say

In the majority of developed countries, middle class people have the dilemma of deciding whether to buy or rent a house. If they live in the United States, Italy, Germany, Ireland, Spain or the UK, then buying is the typical answer. House prices in these countries have almost doubled in the last six years alone. Often people argue that renting is like throwing money away and so it is wiser to repay a mortgage and build equity. However, what if house prices fall? A relatively small adjustment would quickly diminish the equity of numerous home owners. If house price inflation is not set to continue, home ownership becomes less attractive and more people will rent accommodation. Additionally, people are increasingly required to be geographically mobile to advance in their careers. Renting accommodation allows individuals to be more flexible as relocation is easier.

47) The article highlights how homeowners may not always be able to rely on capital growth.

A) True   B) Not True   C) Cannot say

48) The majority of middle class people in developed countries prefer to own their home.

A) True   B) Not True   C) Cannot say

49) You can infer from the article that if house prices stop increasing, fewer people would rent.

A) True   B) Not True   C) Cannot say

50) House prices in Ireland have more than doubled in the last 6 years.

A) True   B) Not True   C) Cannot say

Answers

1	C) - Article does not refer to other types of fraud
2	C) - Article does not state details of the new measures
3	B) - Article states the new measures are not yet in place
4	A) - Article states coursework has made it easier to score top marks
5	C) - No stats given
6	B) - A grades has more than doubled since the previous 10%
7	B) - Article states monetary values are based on survey responses
8	B) - Article says predominantly used after event to assess damage
9	C) - Article only says it is being used increasingly in the health field
10	B) - Article says modern medicine is also concerned with prevention
11	B) - Article mentions successes of medicine centuries ago
12	A) - Article mentions this
13	A) - Article states the radioactive waste is a major drawback
14	A) - Article mentions aesthetic problems of non-renewables
15	C) - Article does not mention this
16	B) - Article says that the effects are a great obstacle to development
17	A) - The migrants' home country is by definition the donor country
18	C) - Article does not mention exactly who emigrates
19	A) - Article says they have tried it
20	A) - Article states blockade was by opposition to government
21	C) - It is not possible to deduce from the article
22	C) - Article doesn't say administrators made their concerns known
23	A) - Article states that fraud is currently rare
24	A) - Article says change has made elections more open to fraud
25	A) - Article states there is a process for checking validity
26	A) - Article says speculative attacks occur when reserves run low
27	C) – Only if the market believes defending the parity will fail
28	B) - Article mentions government have options to avoid attacks
29	B) - Article states traders view
30	A) - You can infer this from the article

31	C) - Article doesn't say whether India and China are net importers
32	C) - We can't infer from article that it controls all
33	A) - Article states brain controls our feelings and emotions
34	C) - This can't be inferred from the article
35	B) - Article says improving efficiency is the cheaper of the options
36	B) - Article says there are no mandatory policies in place
37	A) - Article states that it is not suited to space heating requirements
38	A) - This is an extension of the theory
39	B) - Pop may include many elderly who have not drawn savings
40	C) - Article does not give enough information to draw this conclusion
41	B) - Article says that the visual spectrum is light we can see
42	C) - Article mentions nothing about hearing
43	A) - Article states longer wavelengths have lower energy photons
44	B) - Article states UK pays an inflated rate
45	C) - The article does not provide enough information to say
46	B) - Article states charges sometimes apply for receiving calls
47	A) - Article mentions capital growth is only in certain developed countries
48	C) - Article doesn't mention all developed countries
49	B) - Home ownership should be less attractive so more will rent
50	B) - Article states house prices have almost doubled

PERSONALITY QUESTIONNAIRE

Personality questionnaires are by far the simplest of the tests and as such do not require practice. There are only three things you must note. Firstly, they tend to ask repetitive questions. Sometimes they will ask the same question ten times to see if you are being consistent in your answers. To be consistent you must answer honestly. Secondly, even though you are answering honestly, read the type of character traits the recruiters are looking for and try to form an image of yourself in your mind as that sort of person. Then even though you are answering honestly, you can slightly mould your personality traits to tick their preferred criteria. Finally, try and avoid the extreme answers. Often you are asked to rate your answer on a 1-5 scale, with 3 being indifferent. Keep the majority of your answers as either 2 or 4. Feel free to have the odd truthful extreme answer but make sure it doesn't make you look psychopathic. Also, remember that the personality questionnaire is mainly used to eliminate candidates, rather than as criteria from which to select candidates. You are far less likely to invoke strong emotions from the examiner and so are less likely to be eliminated if you avoid extreme answers.

STAGE 3:

TELEPHONE INTERVIEW
OR
FIRST INTERVIEW

OUTLINE

As so often in life, preparation is crucial. It is difficult to determine the amount of time you should spend preparing for an interview. Indicators include the duration and type of interview – perhaps it is just a competency based interview. Should you be unsure on the interview format, I have created an interview template to prepare you thoroughly, without wasting too much time. After all, if you have performed the online application process proficiently, you will find yourself with a lot of telephone or first interviews. For this reason, spending a huge amount of time researching each company will only take time that could be used to submit extra job applications. In the numbers game, the aim is to pass 90% of the stages and the following format will help you achieve this.

Before your interview, make sure you write answers to the following questions. When you are performing the telephone interview, have them in front of you; along with your stock competency answers from stage one. Should you be invited to a first interview rather than a telephone interview, use the same interview template but refer to the interview techniques section in stage four for information on how to present yourself.

THE INTERVIEW TEMPLATE

What do you know about the company?

Learn four or five facts such as number of employees, turnover, head office location, one recent news event and one interesting fact.

Why do you want to work for the company?

Use the answer you provided in the online application section.

Why do you want to work as a ......?

Use the answer you provided in the online application section.

.

What are the major challenges facing the firm or industry in the future?

Use the internet, specifically the firm's website and www.wikipedia.org to come up with a couple of ideas.

What does the role entail?

It will say this on their website so feel free to regurgitate what they say.

What do you know about the graduate programme?

Again, just regurgitate what they say on their website.

What are the service areas within the company?

Check the website and list the few main areas, briefly explaining what they are.

Who are our major clients?

Just make sure you know 3 or 4 of their largest or most interesting clients.

Who are our competitors?

Avoid obvious flattery such as "your firm is so marvellous they are in a league of their own". Just mention two or three competitors and have a little knowledge on each.

What makes the firm different from its competitors?

Just use the little knowledge from above to pick out the differences. Examples include brand strength, techniques for adding value, corporate responsibility etc.

What are your career objectives?

This is not the time to mention your Hollywood ambitions. Recruiters want to hear that you are ambitious but want to stay at the firm for a considerable time. The best answers will pick out individual positions within the company such as senior marketing executive and mention step by step how you plan to reach this goal. Be slightly overambitious but stay in the realms of what is realistic.

What skills do you have that will make you superior to other candidates?

There should be a list of skills they are looking for on their website. Just mention each skill on there and give a brief example demonstrating it.

Competencies

The most common type of telephone or first interview is mainly concerned with your competencies. To prepare for this, write out the skills the firm desires and provide one example of when you have demonstrated each skill. Make sure you have the competency page at the start of this book to hand so if they ask you for any other skills you can just read one of these examples. If you are attending a face to face interview, you will unfortunately have to learn some extra examples.

Questions to ask

When you ask questions, it is very rare that employers will give you useful answers. The likelihood is they will make vague statements which allow no comparisons to be made between firms, such as "we have an excellent working environment". The aim of this section is not to allow you to compare firms, but to show 'genuine' interest in the firm and demonstrate your knowledge and skills. Just as important as what you ask are your listening skills and how you respond. For example, if they tell you staff turnover is low, keep the conversation flowing by asking them why they think this is. Their answers will mainly be rehearsed but try and continue the conversation to create rapport. If you do create rapport, there is a higher chance they will like you and your application will have a better chance of progression. In the telephone interview stage you should ask fewer questions than in the final interview. Feel free just to ask two or three. Examples of questions to ask are:

- What skill does the firm value most in its employees?
- Are there opportunities to travel?
- What are the levels of staff turnover?
- How is a graduates performance reviewed and how often?
- What is the working atmosphere like?

THORNTONS CHOCOLATES EXAMPLE

The Thorntons chocolates example has been included to illustrate the concept. The template was also used with equal success for a range of applications including blue chip companies such as Accenture, KPMG, JP Morgan and Allianz. However, I have included the Thornton's example as it is slightly less tedious. I suggest writing a template on a computer like the one below and tweaking your answers for the different firms you apply to. I wouldn't recommend writing full answers as it will sound like you are reading out pre-rehearsed answers. It is better to write out bullet points like the ones below. When they ask you questions, refer to these and answer them by expanding on the bullet points. Make sure you also have your sheet of competency questions to hand.

What do you know about the company?

- Established by Joe Thornton in 1911 in Sheffield
- 180m turnover with 400 shops and 200 franchises
- 36% rise in profit this year to £7.1m
- In 1996 Thorntons planned to open 100 new stores but was over-ambitious
- Steady improvement in the last few years since the unsuccessful proposed buy-out

Why do you want to work for the company?

- Market leader in food manufacturing
- Responsibility, playing a key part in the sourcing of £24m budget
- Not a huge company so what I do will be noticed
- The opportunity to learn cutting edge innovative skills in buying and negotiating
- Expanding industry as health awareness is causing people to eat quality over quantity

Why do you want to work as a buyer?

- Opportunity to work in a constantly changing environment is exciting
- Sourcing new products is exciting
- It was the favourite aspect of my job when working at Henley House

What are the major challenges facing the firm or industry in the future?

- Gift delivery service
- Online low cost firms such as Hotel Chocolat

What does the role entail?

A buyer purchases the highest quality goods at the lowest cost, making sure the goods bought meet the demands of the customer in terms of both quantity and quality. The work involves:

- Analysing market trends

- Reviewing performance indicators and sales
- Meeting suppliers and negotiating

What do you know about the graduate programme?

2 year modular based programme with the opportunity to work in various service areas

What are our service areas?

- Gift delivery
- Thornton's cafes
- Thornton's retail outlets
- Internet services

What are your career objectives?

I aim to be a senior buyer within 5 years. One of the reasons I applied to a medium size company rather than the blue chip companies is that my work will be more transparent and I will be given real responsibility from an early stage of my career so there will be an opportunity to progress quickly.

Who are our competitors?

Hotel Chocolat, Green and black, Lindt, Amelie, Neuhaus, Leonidas.

What makes the firm different from its competitors?

Known for quality ingredients and elusive recipes

What skills do you have that make you superior to other candidates?

- Excellent communicator: Demonstrated as assistant manager at Henley House and training new workers at Heathrow Airport
- High level of analytical skills and numerical skills: Economics degree
- Confident negotiator and commitment to quality: Negotiated with Dinos as hall football captain and negotiated with hotels on sponsored cycle ride

Questions to ask

- How is a graduate's performance reviewed and how often?
- Does Thorntons place emphasis on staff training?
- What is the working atmosphere like?
- Where do you see the company in 5 years?
- What are the most probable career routes from this position?

STAGE 4:

ASSESSMENT CENTRE

OUTLINE

The assessment day was introduced to improve the accuracy of the recruitment process by using many recruiters and many tasks to get a more comprehensive view of the candidates' abilities. Assessment days have various formats but every one incorporates many or all of the following components:

- The welcome
- Interview
- Case study
- Presentation
- Lunch / break
- Group exercise
- Role play

It is possible that recruiters will save the psychometric testing for the assessment day but this is rare and they will warn you if this is the case. Other assessment days will have two or three interviews instead of one. The format for the day is unimportant; what is important is that you contact the firm's Human Resources department beforehand to find out what activities you will take part in so you can prepare. This section of the book will focus on how to excel in all of the above tasks so you will be ready for any assessment day format.

Soft skills

The assessment centre is designed to differentiate candidates based on their soft skills. Soft skills are intangible characteristics such as leadership, creativity and the ability to work in a team. Whilst you will likely have been required to give examples of your soft skills in the application section, the assessment day requires you to demonstrate them. The common view of both recruiters and preachers is that soft skills are a part of your personality so difficult to learn. Wonderfully, this is just another misconception. Just as actors can adjust their soft skills to play various characters, players can adjust their soft skills to meet the needs of various employers.

It is a competition

Unless psychometric tests are included, every aspect of the assessment day is subjective and based completely on the assessors' views. Unlike academic results that produce a measurable score for your abilities – your scores are assigned. The marks you receive are not only subjective but relative as candidates are constantly compared to each other, and to the hiring standard.

Recruiters say things like "we don't have a fixed number of places so all those good enough will be hired". This spiel may be bought by preachers, but it should not be bought by you. After all, if performance is relative, how you do is related to how others do. For the majority of roles, employers are looking to fast track you into becoming future leaders. Consequently, when engaging in the group discussion, it doesn't matter how well you do; if you are not one of the leaders, you will not be hired. Equally, if the person presenting before you performed brilliantly, your presentation will look inferior. Make no mistake about the fact that you are competing.

BEFORE THE DAY

There are stories of people who take preparation so far that they actually go and sit outside the company's office all day to learn details such as what people wear, what people have for lunch and what time they leave. You will be pleased to note that all this is unnecessary. Don't even think about doing this – life is just too short. By submitting numerous applications you not only increase the number of potential jobs you could be offered, you reduce the importance of each job. This in turn will reduce the level of stress on the day, further enhancing your chance of success.

Aside from reading this chapter, to prepare for an assessment day you should:

- Learn the interview template and competency stories
- Prepare you appearance
- Plan your route
- Prepare your state of mind

The interview template and competency stories

Before your assessment day you should create an interview template to help you answer the majority of questions you are likely to encounter. Unlike when preparing for the telephone interview, you will actually have to learn your template. Of course, there is no need to learn it word for word, but try and remember a few key points for each potential question. Unless you are really quick thinking and have numerous stories from which to highlight your competencies, I suggest you think of examples of when you have demonstrated particular skills. If you can find out the specific skills a firm is looking for, you should write them down and remember an example of a time in which you have demonstrated each one.

Your appearance

In order to act the part, you must look the part. You should make honest judgements on your physical appearance and decide what to wear. The best advice is to just try and fit in with the firm without wearing anything you are too uncomfortable in. Please don't use these occasions to make fashion statements and try out your latest white shoes and pink sock combination. For the vast majority of graduate jobs, males should wear suits and females should wear smart office attire. If you are applying to a modern, young and innovative firm, you may be able to tone down your clothing. It is important that you feel comfortable in the clothes you pick. You may have the smartest suit in the world but if you don't feel comfortable, you will not seem confident and the impression you make will be inferior.

Whether we like to admit it or not, recruiters will have a range of prejudices. Other than prejudices against age, gender and race, exist prejudices against characteristics such as jewellery, facial hair, weight and height. If you are overweight, wear dark flattering clothes. If you have a beard or unruly hair, have a shave and smarten up. Once you get the job you can always go back to your old habits. While they might not hire you if you have a goatee, they will not fire you for growing one. So comply with society's central ground and try not to offend anyone. You might feel like you don't want to work for a firm that discriminates against your 'designer stubble'. I fully empathise with your concerns. However, these are the concerns of a preacher; a player will do whatever it takes to get the job, leaving the choice of whether to accept it to a later date.

Plan your route

Obviously, make sure you check the exact dates and times of your assessment days and be punctual. I have a rare aptitude for getting to assessment centres within a couple of minutes of the start time. Please avoid following my example as getting there on time usually involved a 2 mile sprint with a heavy bag on my back. Spending the first ten minutes of the day concentrating solely on breathing is not an ideal start. Another common mistake is that graduates receive assessment day offers but fail to confirm their attendance – please don't do this.

Prepare your state of mind

Once you have arrived at the assessment centre you must get into the player persona – the persona of the 'perfect' candidate for the job. The aim is to look and feel confident and relaxed.

To help you speak in a relaxed manner you must relax your jaw, throat, shoulders, arms and abdomen. To relax your abdomen, breathe out as much as you can, then breathe in through your nose, hold, and breathe out through your mouth. Making your hands into fists as tight as you can and holding for a few seconds before releasing quickly will loosen the arms. The shoulders can be relaxed by rolling them backwards and forwards a few times in each direction. Finally, relax your face and throat by taking a big yawn and opening your mouth as wide as possible. Executing these exercises in private would be prudent!

It is not enough to be relaxed, you must also feel confident. Every feeling we ever have is caused by a thought. For example, we don't just feel nervous, we feel nervous because thoughts run through our mind like: if I screw up this presentation, I will look like a fool. Fortunately, we can easily change our feelings, just by changing our thoughts. You should visualise yourself as a powerful, impressive figure that is certain to get the job. The effects of visualisations can be reinforced by complementing them with affirmations which require you to repeat a few positive sentences either aloud or in your head to block out any negative thoughts. Upon completing these short mental and physical exercises, you should feel calm and confident. You will then be ready to enter the assessment centre.

THE WELCOME

The day will typically start with each candidate introducing themselves and telling everyone a little about their background. Most candidates will thrill you with the news of where they are from and what course they do. While this may be good enough for Jeremy Paxman, it will not impress the recruiters. Try and say something interesting or different to help distinguish yourself.

Next, a recruiter will give you a presentation on the firm. This is the time to learn some of the facts you couldn't find on the internet. If possible, write them down so you can learn them before your interview. At the end of the presentation which usually lasts fifteen minutes, be prepared to ask questions. You do not need to deliver the world's most insightful question, just come up with 2 or 3 reasonable questions. Make sure you ask them as soon as you get the opportunity, otherwise someone else may ask your question, or the fear of breaking the silence will build so much that you say nothing. I've been there.

THE INTERVIEW

In the interview you will be assessed on:

- Your motivations for working at the firm
- Your key competencies
- Your technical knowledge and business acumen

On the majority of occasions there will be just one interview that covers your motivations, knowledge of the job and your key competencies and skills. Alternatively, you might have two or three interviews with ostentatious labels like aspirational interview (motivations), specialist interview (technical knowledge) and differentiator interview (key competencies). Don't be confused by their ridiculous titles - they all encompass these same three aspects and luckily for you, so does the interview template. If you have solid answers to all the template questions and have learnt your competency answers, you should have more than enough knowledge to pass all of the three interviews.

Use the interview template

The interview should be treated very similarly to the telephone interview, with the only differences being that they are generally longer and are in person. By all means, feel free to gain more knowledge about the firm and industry than the template demands but this is unlikely to be necessary. It is always possible that you will encounter questions that are not in the template. If this is the case, don't panic - you do not need to provide perfect answers. Providing satisfactory or even slightly below average answers should be acceptable as you will have given beautiful answers to the questions outlined in the template.

Your level of expertise

If you are applying for a technical role, please attempt to learn some of the technical vocabulary. You do not need to be a guru as most firms are looking for individuals with potential rather than the finished article. If they wanted an expert in accountancy, they would get an already trained accountant, not a graduate. However, learning some technical vocabulary will impress recruiters as it evinces interest and commitment to your chosen field.

The first impression

There is little debate on the importance of your first impression. If you start badly it may be possible to turn the interview around but it is certainly going to be difficult. In contrast, start strongly, build rapport and the interview may just be a breeze. So how do you create a good first impression? Dress smartly, walk in the room with your head and shoulders held back, maintain eye contact, smile and give a strong handshake. As you shake the interviewer's hand, introduce yourself and remember the interviewer's name – simple! If you struggle to do any of the above, go out into a public venue and practice introducing yourself to internalise the process.

Ultimately, the impact you make will be out of your hands – maybe the employer discriminates against women or feels threatened by tall men. The point is that you can't control the recruiters' first impression, but by following the wonderfully simple points above, you will undoubtedly enhance your prospects of making it positive.

Body language

Some candidates waste time learning advanced body language techniques to try and help them in their interview. They learn techniques such as mirroring your breathing, tonality and speed of speech to your interviewer to create rapport. While these techniques may be valid, rather than give you the edge, they are likely to overwhelm you with information and reduce the impact of your performance. If you have reasonable interpersonal skills you can pass the majority of interviews without learning these elaborate techniques.

The problem is that even simple body language techniques are difficult to remember in the heat of an interview. You have to remember to smile, gesture slowly, sit upright, maintain eye contact, speak clearly, contemplate the questions before answering etc. Rather than remembering all these body language techniques, all you need to remember are the two core activities that elicit them.

You should concentrate on breathing slowly from the diaphragm and maintaining a good posture by sitting up straight with you head and shoulders back – as demonstrated by the Alexander technique. These two simple techniques not only give the impression that you are calm and confident, they make you feel it. You will automatically smile, maintain eye contact, speak clearly, listen to the questions carefully and spend longer contemplating your answers. Armed with the simple posture and breathing techniques, and the content on the interview template, you can pass 90% of your interviews without the risk of freaking out recruiters by mirroring their every movement.

THE CASE STUDY

The case study will require you to look at a business problem and come up with a solution. You are assessed on:

- Your ability to think quickly
- Your ability to solve problems
- Your ability to analyse information and focus on the key issues
- Your ability to work with limited information

You will typically receive a booklet containing various mediums of information, such as accounts or emails. While the length of the booklet can vary considerably, ranging from a few pages to whole booklet, one constant is that there is rarely one correct answer. To really master the case studies, make sure you read your task and the introduction particularly carefully. Even though you

are working against the clock, take time to analyse the situation before attempting to make notes or answer the questions.

The case studies are designed to be difficult to prepare for, allowing recruiters to judge all candidates from a level playing field. The best way to gain a competitive advantage is to practice doing a case study and examine the style of answers the recruiters are looking for. The following website provides a typical case study to practice and most importantly, provides feedback:

- http://www.bcg.com/careers/interactive_splash.html

THE PRESENTATION

While performing a presentation you will be assessed on:

- The content
- Your delivery
- Your ability to field questions

The content

Unless you are told to prepare your presentation prior to the assessment day, there is little preparation you can do to improve its content. What you can do is learn the basics for producing a powerful presentation. Since an audience's concentration is highest at the start and end, try and emphasise your key points in these sections. Additionally, make sure your presentation is divided into three topics as this has proved the most effective in maintaining an audience's attention.

The quality of the content in your presentation will also be affected by the notes you use. While having more notes would suggest your content will be superior, it will also reduce the impact of your delivery. The best compromise can be achieved by using prompt cards and adopting the 4 x 4 rule – a maximum of 4 bullet points and 4 words per bullet point on each card. Minimising the information to bullets or key words gives you a greater opportunity to engage with your audience.

Your delivery

The delivery of your presentation incorporates both verbal and non-verbal communication. As with the interview, they can be improved by adopting a good posture and breathing deeply to give you a calm and confident manner. However, there are two main differences from your interview.

Firstly, you will likely be standing and secondly, you will be speaking for a greater length of time. To create a good impression whilst standing, just make sure you stand still and avoid any rocking movements. Speaking for a longer period requires you to maintain an audience's attention by talking loudly, pausing and emphasising key words.

Speaking loudly, clearly and in short sentences helps maintain energy in your voice. By directing your words to the back of the room, you will come across with greater strength and purpose. Whenever you feel tension in your voice, increase the volume to create energy, hide shakiness and grab the attention of your audience.

Pausing at the end of your sentences enable you to take a breath, slow down the speed of your delivery and give yourself chance to think of what you are going to say. A pause will also stop you using filler words like "um" or "er" which make you look nervous and unprofessional. To further distinguish your performance from others, avoid speaking in a monotone by emphasising key words to make your presentation more interesting.

Fielding questions

There is little you can do to prepare for the questions as their content is unknown. Just make sure you take your time to consider the questions, and the answers recruiters want, before responding. Recruiters are going to pick flaws in your presentation. It is fine to accept there are errors as long as you come up with suitable solutions as to how the problems could be overcome, or how you could do it differently next time.

LUNCH / BREAK

It is likely that you will have a break for lunch or drinks at some point during the assessment day. Alternatively, there may be time in which graduates who have recently joined the company will come and talk to you. Naturally, recruiters will 'inadvertently' get you to drop your guard by telling you that you will not be assessed in this period. Of course, this is another misleading statement. While you are not being assessed, what you say and how you act will affect their judgements of you, which in turn affect their assessments. Unfortunately, this means that you can't just relax and enjoy a break from the relentless assessment day. The player must not lose sight of the candidate the recruiters are looking for and as such should endeavour to demonstrate that they are that candidate by asking a range of questions.

Engage in light conversation

The comparatively informal situation allows you to ask much more light hearted questions - after all, you are supposed to be on a break. However, make sure your questions demonstrate the correct undertones. You are trying to give the impression that you are interested in knowing more about the firm, not just because you would like to work there, but because you are comparing them to your alternative options – the social proof of having options is extremely powerful as recruiters don't like to feel they are losing candidates to their rivals. I would suggest asking the following questions:

- How long have you worked here?
- Did you always want to work here?
- What attracted you to the firm?
- What have you been involved in so far?
- What do you expect to be involved in, in the future?
- Do you enjoy working here?
- What do you enjoy about it?
- Is there a vibrant graduate scene within the company?
- What are the major challenges of the graduate scheme?

Don't feel like you have to learn all these questions and recite them one by one - instead use them to initiate a conversation. You will make a good impression by asking a few questions, listening to their answers and keeping the conversation flowing. Having a conversation, rather than a question and answer session not only creates rapport, but gives the impression that your interest in the firm is genuine.

THE GROUP EXERCISE

Group exercises come in a range of formats which require you to work in a team to find a solution to a particular problem. You will be assessed on:

- How well you follow the task instructions
- Your level of contribution to the team effort
- Your leadership skills
- Your ability to listen and communicate with the team
- How you critically evaluate both the performance of yourself and the team

Group exercises vary from building towers using only paper and tape, to sitting in a group and discussing ideas for a local charity. Whether you are actually working together to build something or simply discussing ideas is unimportant as the assessment criteria are identical. Interestingly, the outcome of your challenge is for the main part irrelevant. In fact, some challenges are designed to make you fail to see how you work in the face of adversity.

Following instructions

To demonstrate that you follow task instructions make sure firstly that what you say is specific to achieving the goal and secondly, guide others. Since people will talk just to receive attention, there will be many occasions when people's comments are unrelated to achieving the specific goals. In these circumstances you should say something like "that's a good point James but I think we should try and stick to the main issues". This is a perfect way of politely guiding the conversation and winning kudos both in terms of following instructions and guiding others. To maximise the effect of this comment, aim it at an individual who you sense is particularly annoying the group. By correcting the 'common enemy', the group will see you as a leader – a competency assessors look for.

Your contribution

The quality of what you say is more important than the sheer volume. However, contrary to what recruiters suggest, they offer far more jobs to the confident, loud people that contribute the most. While you don't have to say the lion's share, if you are not contributing at least as much as the average person, you are not contributing enough.

Leading the group

While on most cases, you are not required to be the leader to get the job, it is generally a desirable position to take. To be a leader you should either be physically dominant or verbally dominant. If you have excellent body language or are physically impressive such as a beautiful girl or a well-built male, you may naturally become the leader. If you are neither of the above, you can become the physical leader by positioning yourself at the centre of the group, such as in the middle of a line or at the head of the table and people will subconsciously treat you as the leader. Alternatively, you can be the leader through being verbally dominant, either by saying the most or making the most high quality contributions. People will then naturally look to you to make decisions. This can be enhanced by guiding and including others with comments like "what do you think Jane" or "excellent point Sophie".

Listening & Communicating

To improve your listening try remembering people's names and what they say so you can comment on them. The additional advantage is this makes you look like the leader as you are discussing other people's ideas. To improve your communication skills, practice speaking in a loud and clear voice so other people listen to you without interrupting. Obviously you don't want to be shouting at your group, but speaking in a loud, succinct manner shows confidence and will impress assessors.

Your critical evaluation

Usually you will be asked to evaluate yourself and your team's performance. Try and come up with a few suggestions on how both you and your team could have improved without getting too personal. For example, I would say things like "I found that people often lost track of the goal and I should have helped guide them back to the key issues". Unless your group performance was outstanding, refrain from focusing on the positives as this gives the impression that average is good enough to you. By looking at how you can improve the negatives, you are suggesting that excellence is what you strive for.

THE ROLE PLAY

In the role play you will be assessed on:

- Your ability to listen and communicate
- Your ability to construct arguments
- Your negotiation skills

The role play is the least common of the assessment day tasks and can be based on any topic so is difficult to practice beforehand. For these reasons, a player should not waste time trying to prepare for them. Reading the following paragraph should suffice.

Like the case study, you should try and pick out the key issues and concentrate on them. Remember the desired outcome of the exercise and endeavour to achieve it or get as close to achieving it as possible. A player will listen to what the assessor is saying, communicate their ideas effectively and use negotiation skills to come up with a satisfactory solution.

FINAL THOUGHT

Due to the extremely competitive nature of the recruitment process, you are likely to fail at some point. How you deal with this failure is crucial. Since preachers concentrate on projecting themselves, failure is a reflection on their character, so is a painful experience. After a few failures they will become demoralised, assume they are not the type of person recruiters are looking for and will quit. On the other hand, as a player, you understand it is all just a game and realise that failure is not a personal attack, but an indicator that your skills need improvement. Every time you fail you will analyse your mistakes and make sure you don't repeat them – that way your skills will improve with every application. The more you treat the process as a game, the more you will understand it and the better you will get at playing.

When nothing seems to help, I go and look at a stonecutter hammering away at his rock perhaps a hundred times without as much as a crack showing in it. Yet at the hundred and first blow it will split in two, and I know it was not that blow that did it - but all that had gone before.

Jacob Riis

The Online Supplement

To complement this book, I have created a website to allow readers to share their stories. As well as learning techniques from this book, you can now learn from the successes and failures of others. The website will also enable you to help prepare for specific job interviews and assessment days. Imagine the advantage of talking to someone who has been on your upcoming assessment day.

www.playing-the-graduate-game.com